NESTING GROUNDS

POEMS AND PAINTINGS BY

SARAH JANE CONKLIN

Nesting Grounds
Copyright © 2019 by Sarah Jane Conklin

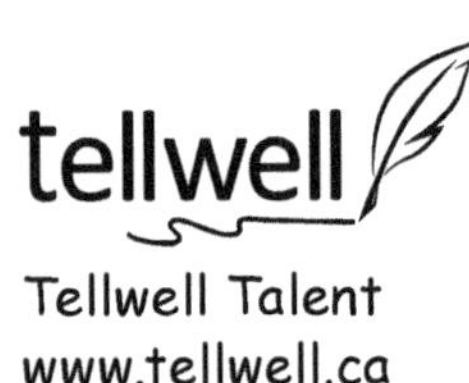

Tellwell Talent
www.tellwell.ca

ISBN
978-0-2288-1706-2 (Paperback)

For the nurturers in my family who always make room in
the bird's nest.

The Nest

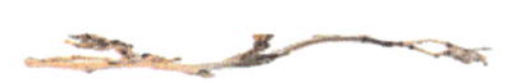

Small twigs and bark, with grass and weeds,
Are weaved into a round.
Then moss and leaves cushion the clutch,
This is the nesting ground.
This cradle is securely built,
In boxes, trees, or ledges.
The female sits and incubates,
With hope her young brood fledges.
Together, couples build their nest,
To keep eggs safe and dry.
Once hatched, they guard and feed their young,
Until they learn to fly.

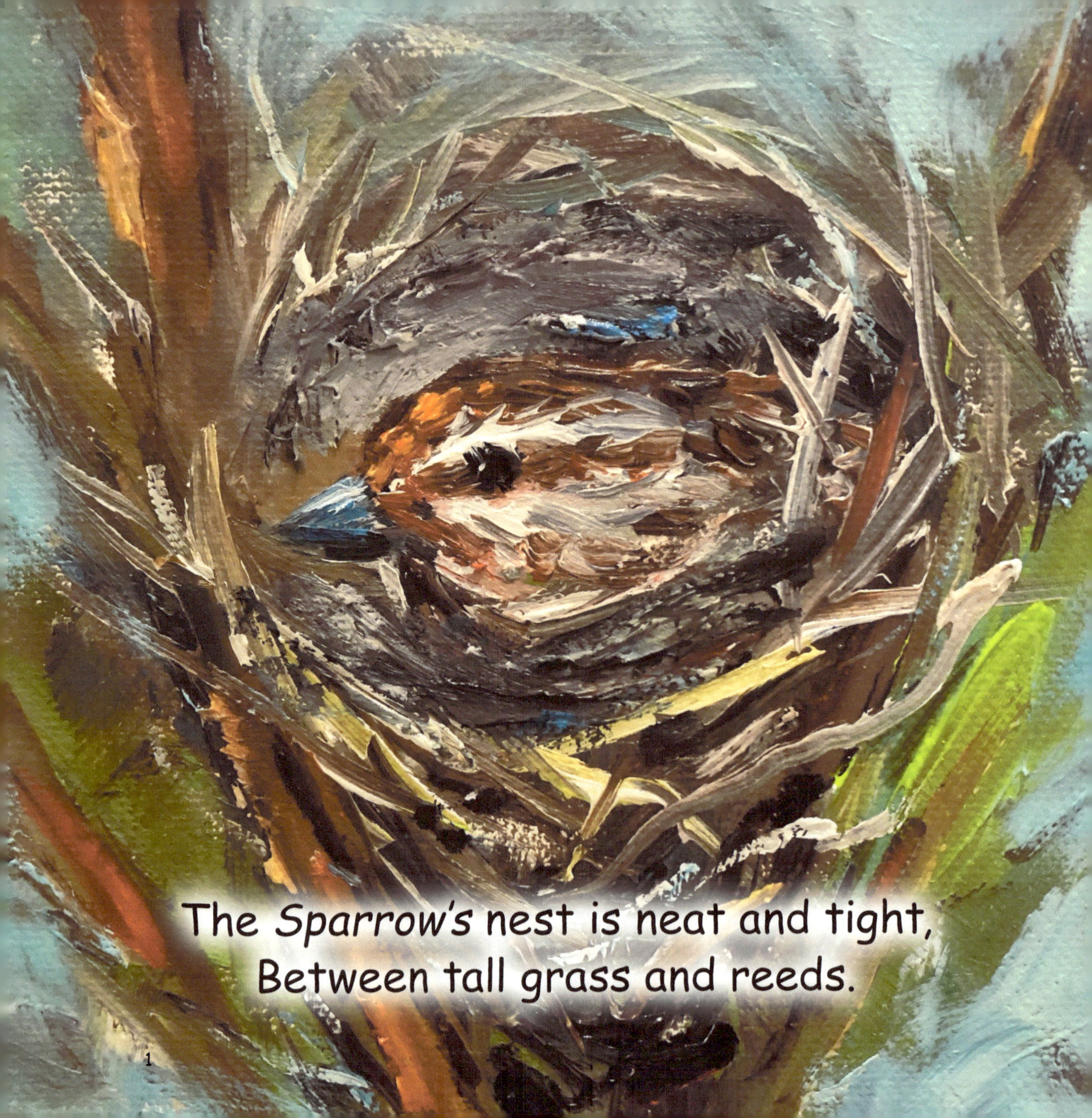
The *Sparrow's* nest is neat and tight,
Between tall grass and reeds.

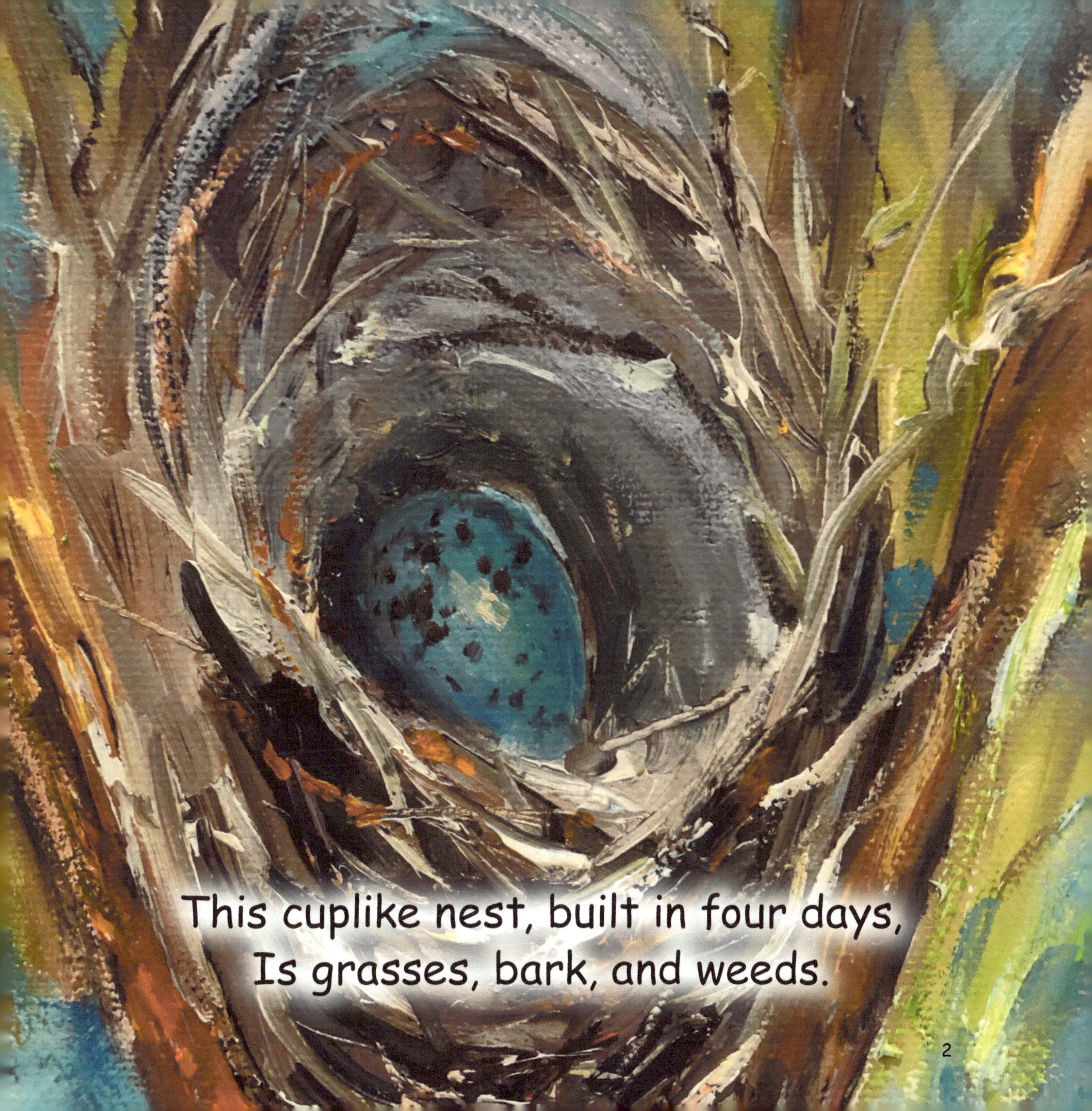

This cuplike nest, built in four days,
Is grasses, bark, and weeds.

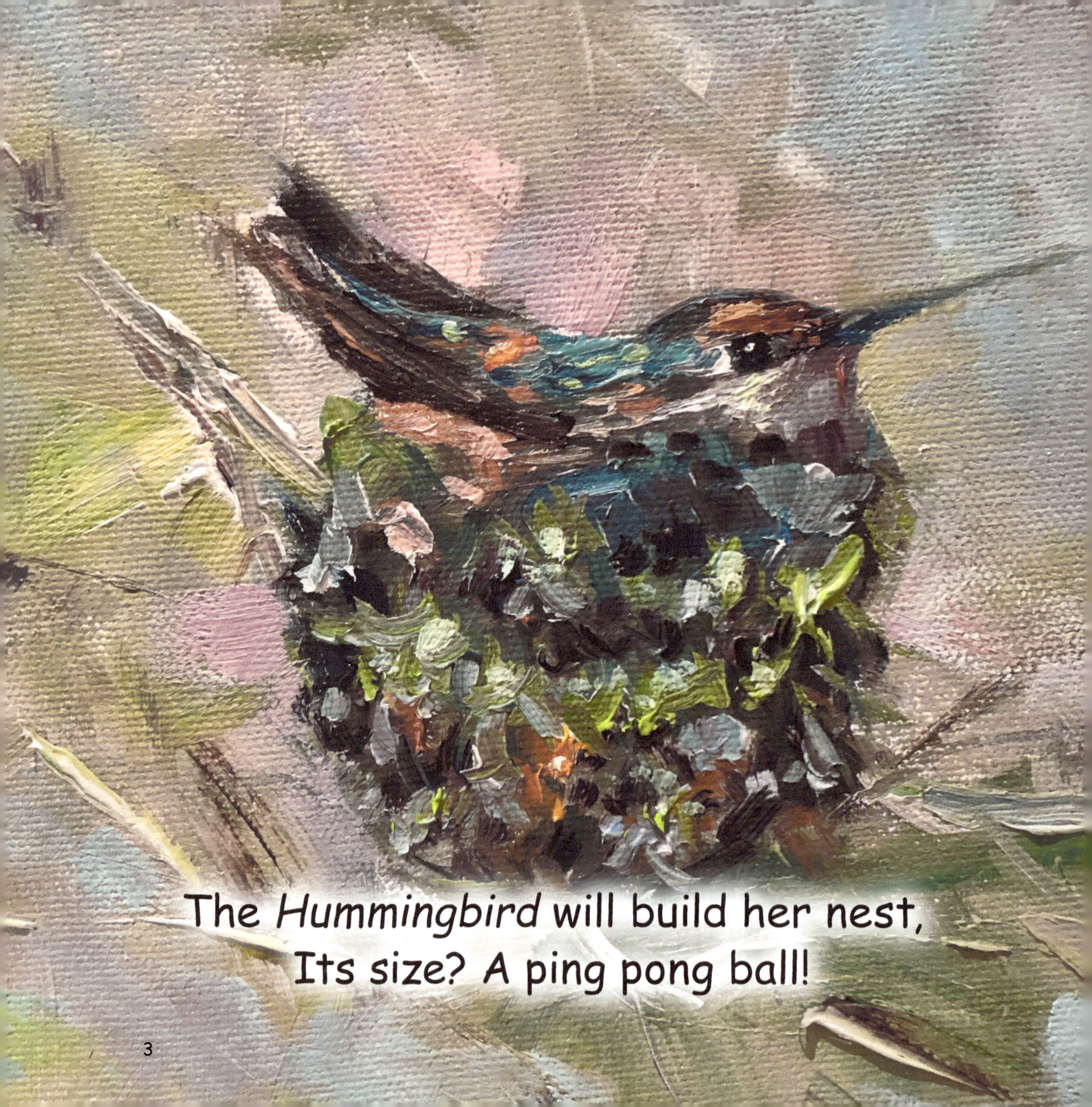

The *Hummingbird* will build her nest,
Its size? A ping pong ball!

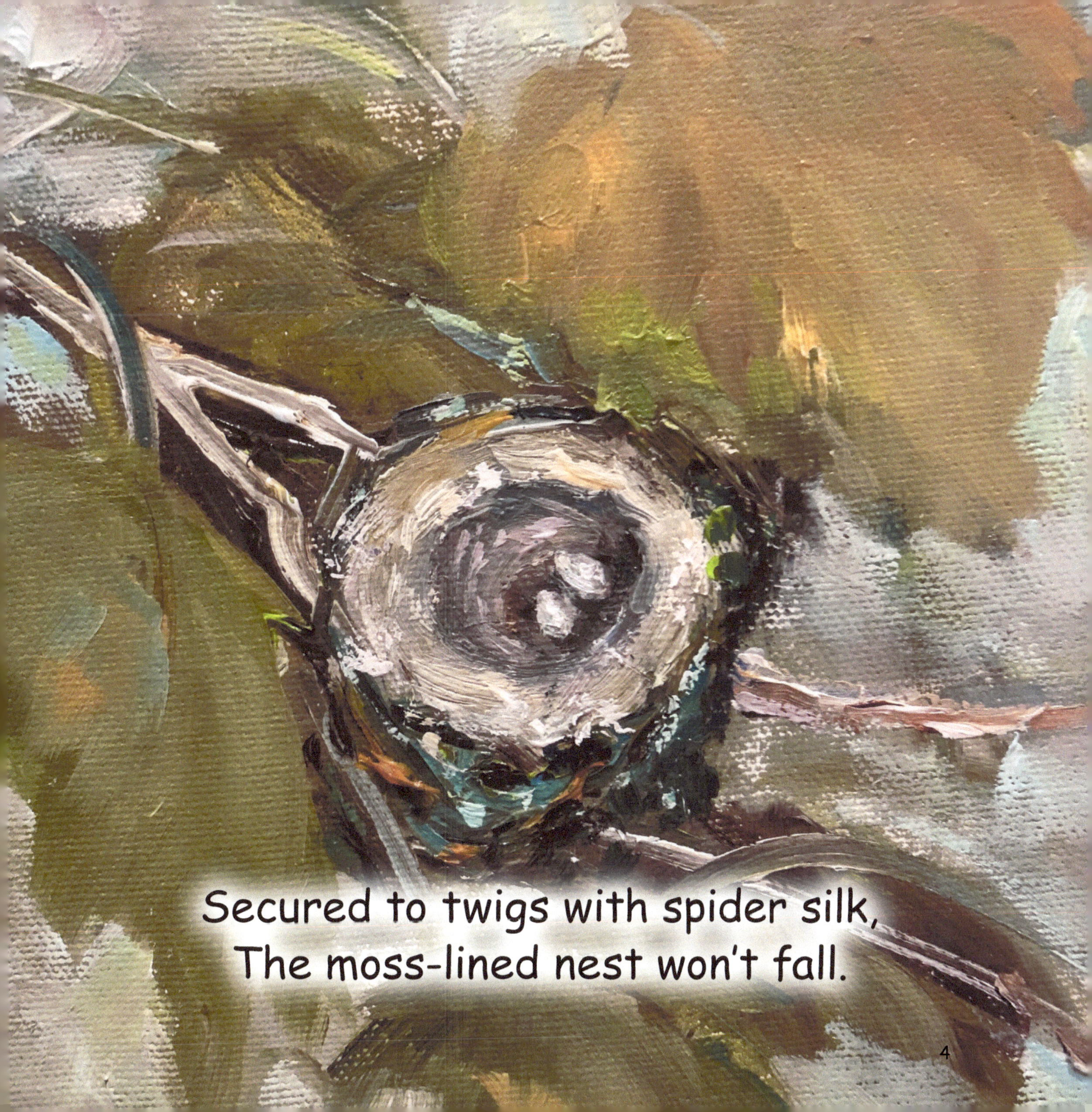
Secured to twigs with spider silk,
The moss-lined nest won't fall.

4

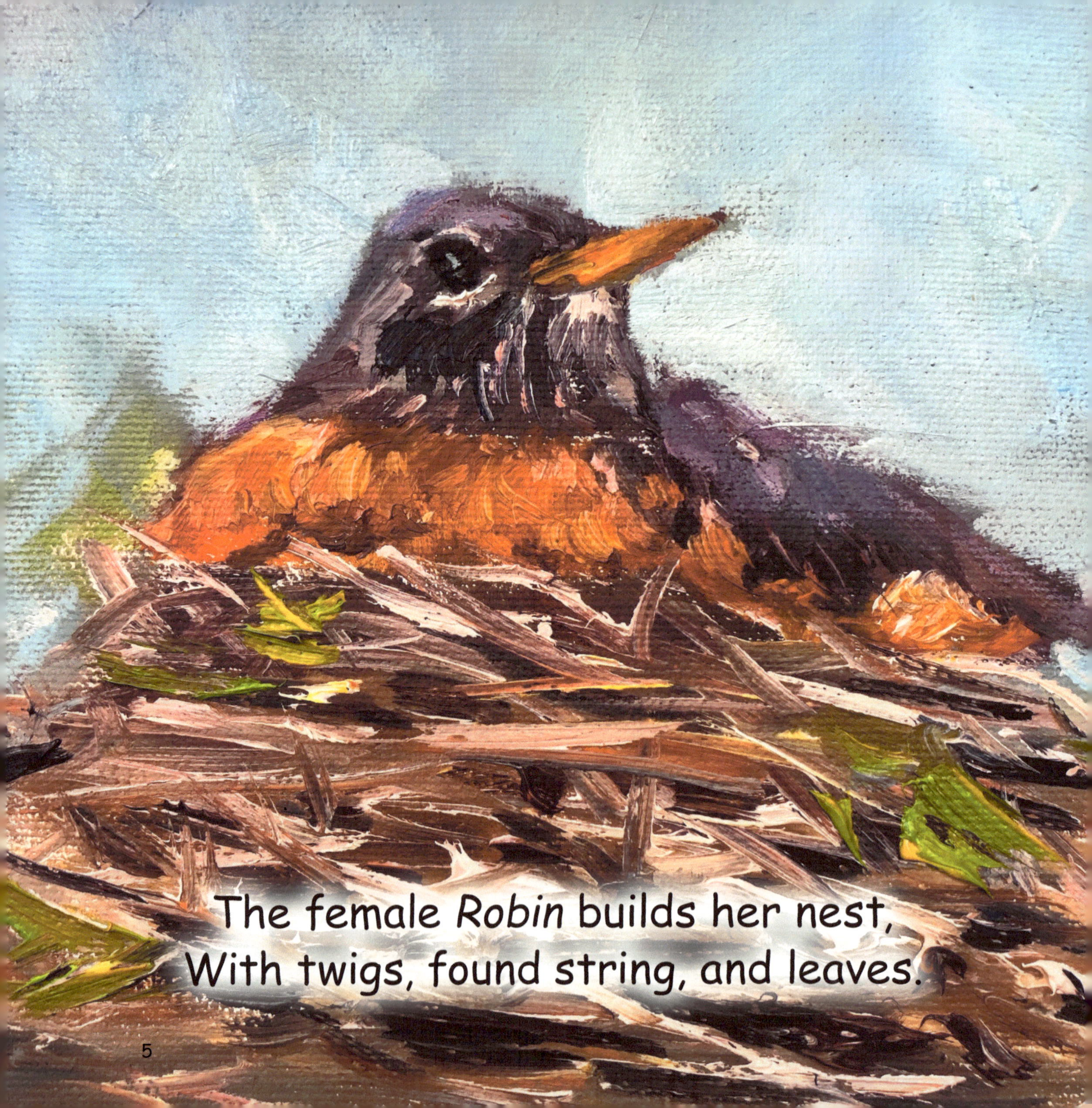
The female *Robin* builds her nest,
With twigs, found string, and leaves.

5

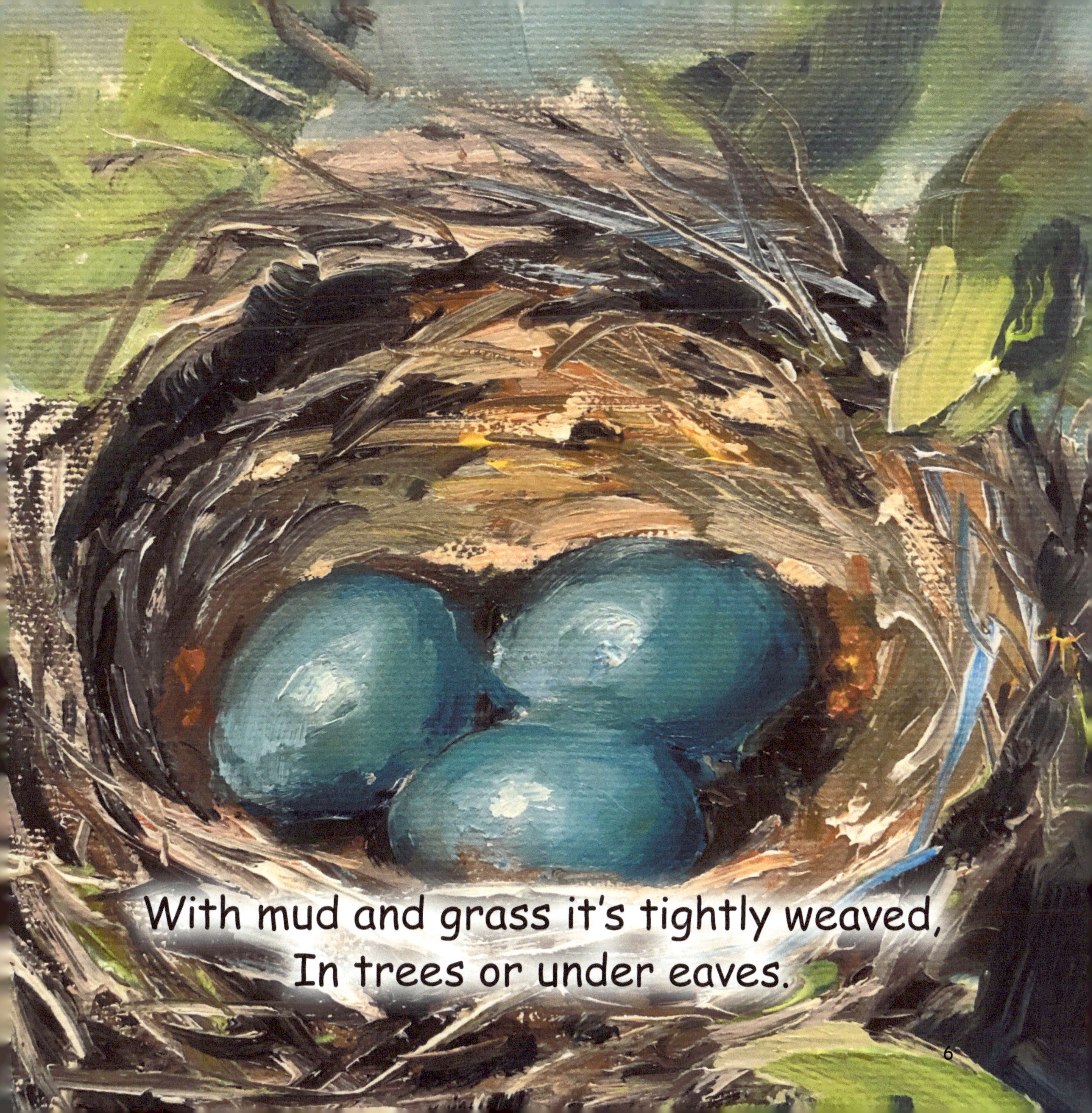

With mud and grass it's tightly weaved,
In trees or under eaves.

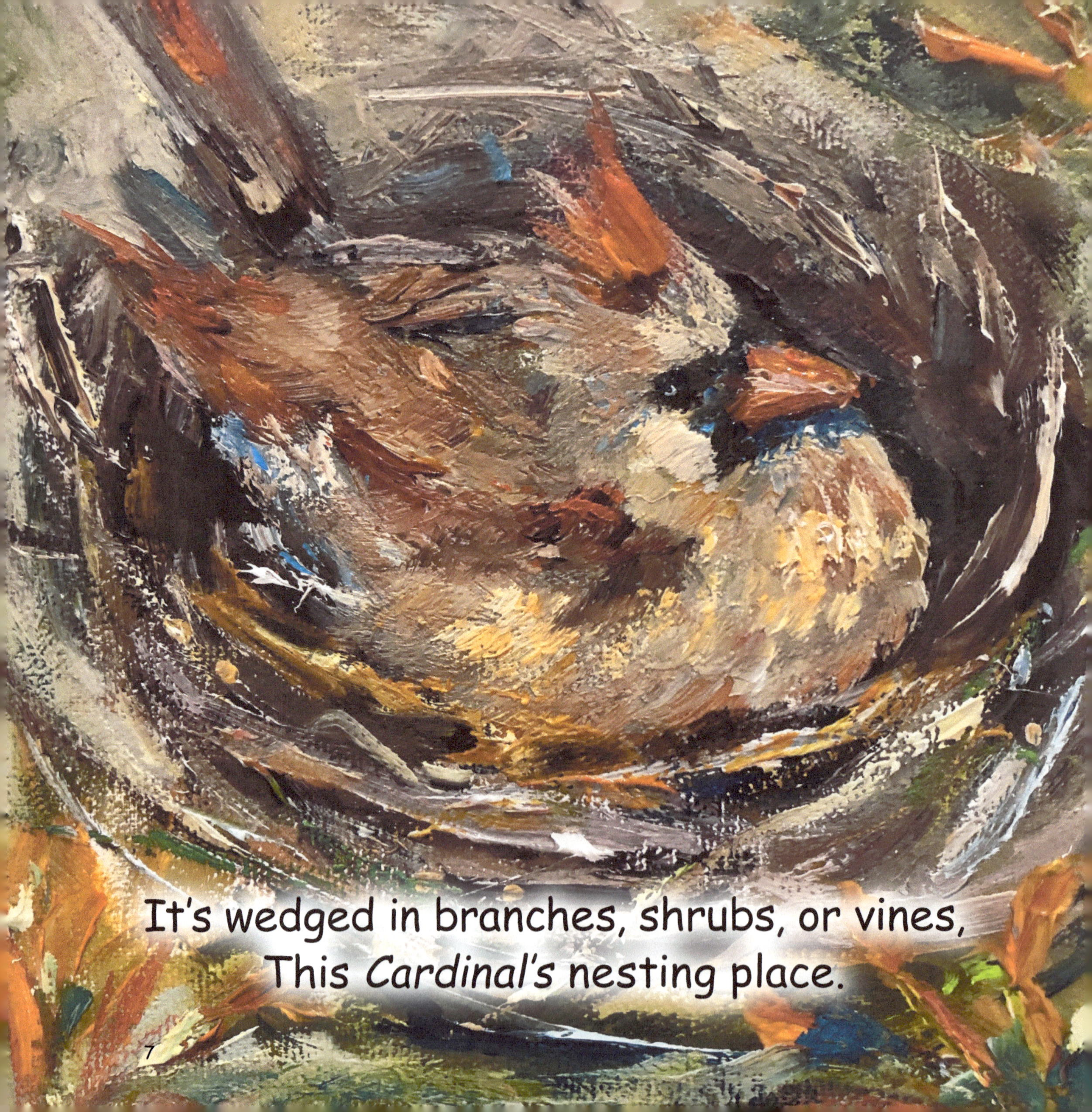
It's wedged in branches, shrubs, or vines,
This *Cardinal's* nesting place.

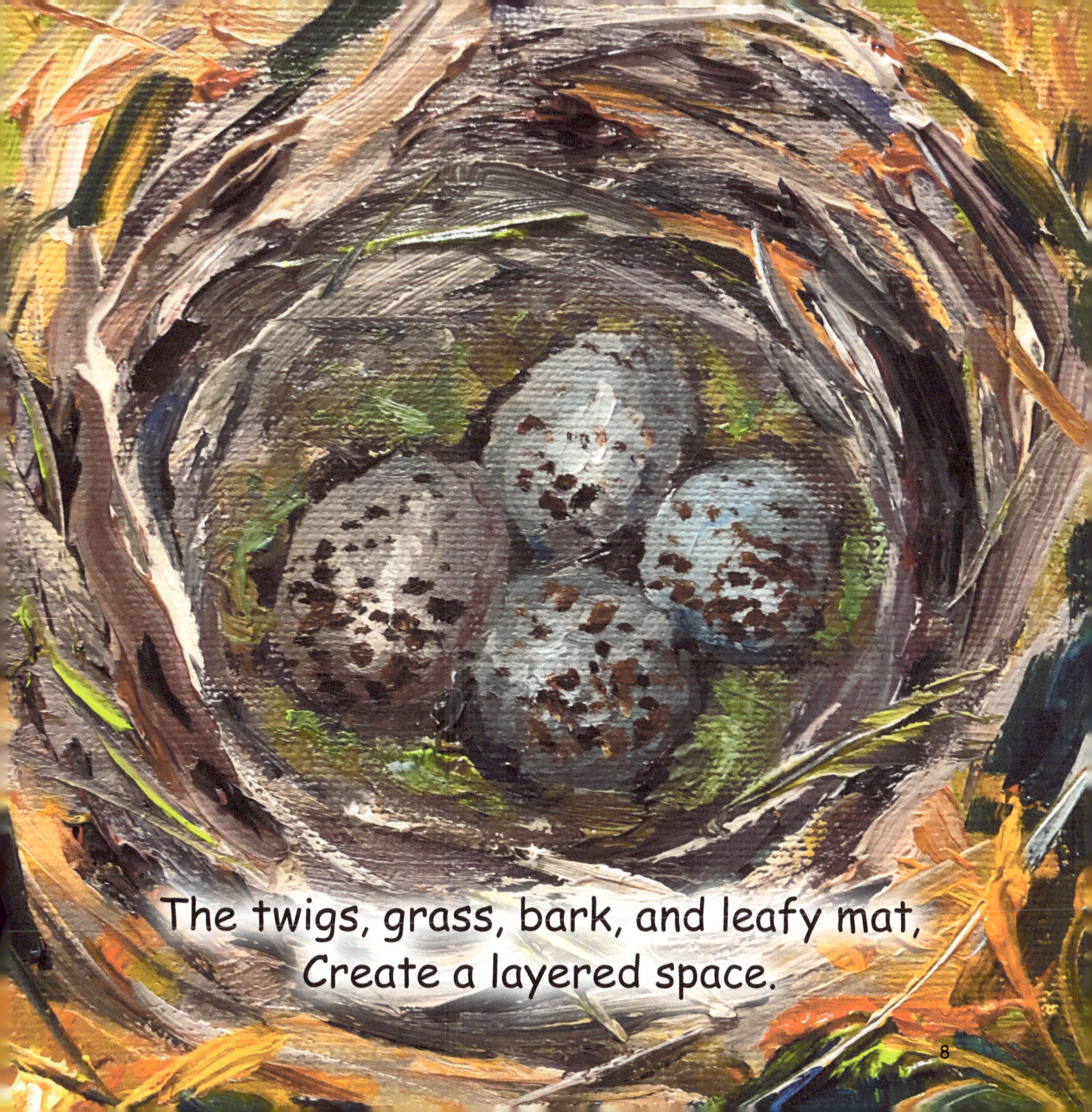

The twigs, grass, bark, and leafy mat,
Create a layered space.

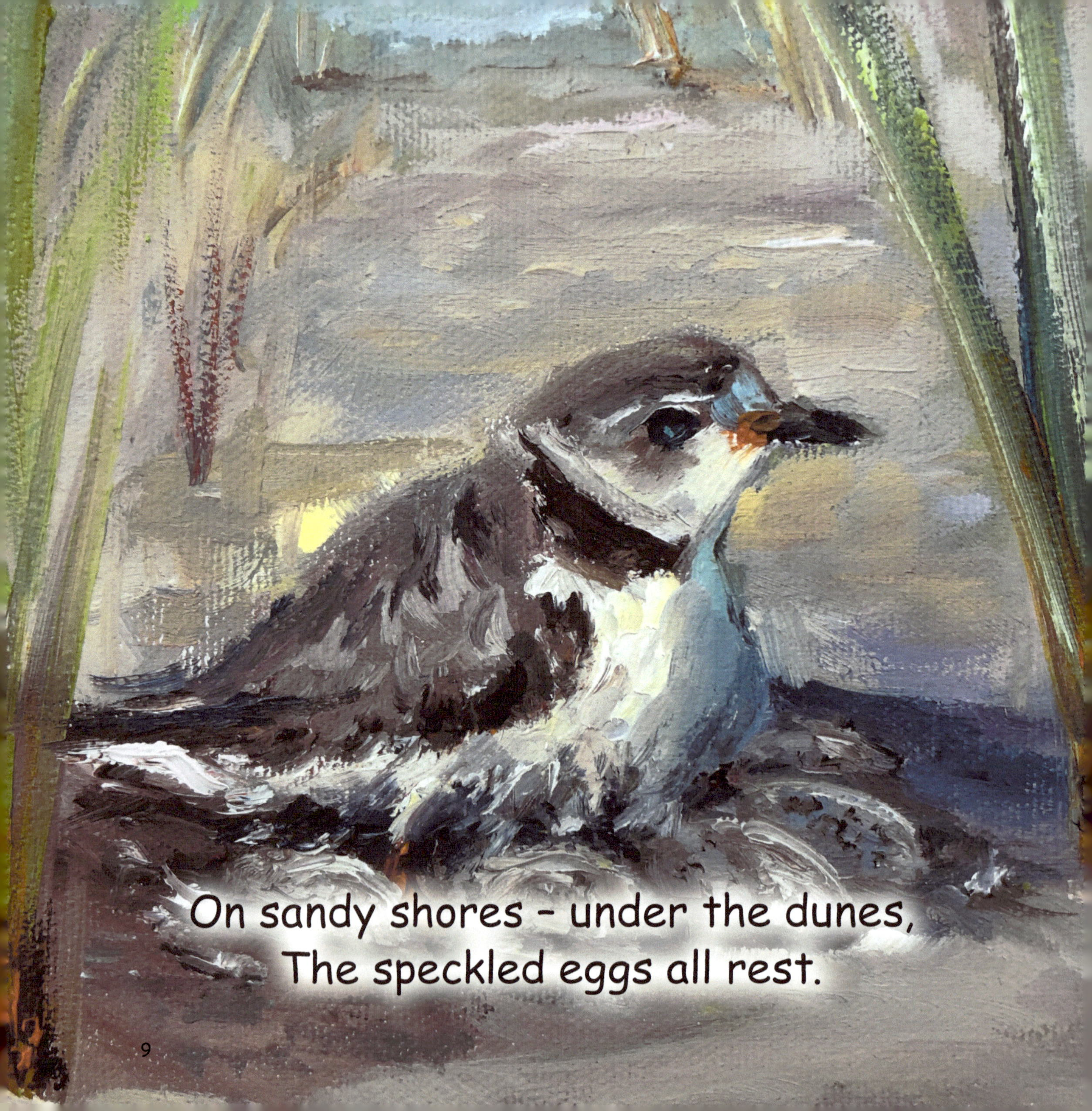

9

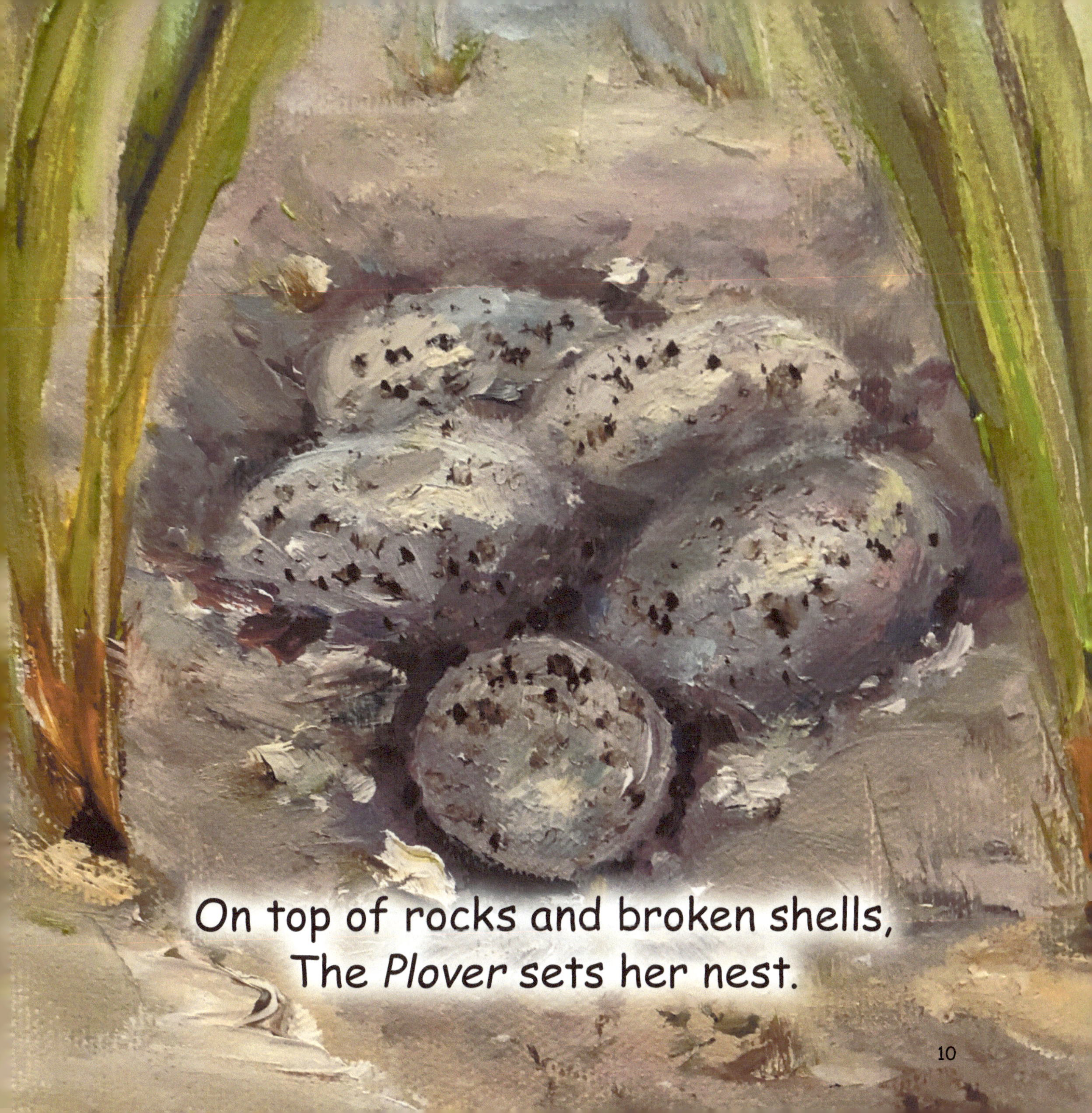

On top of rocks and broken shells,
The *Plover* sets her nest.

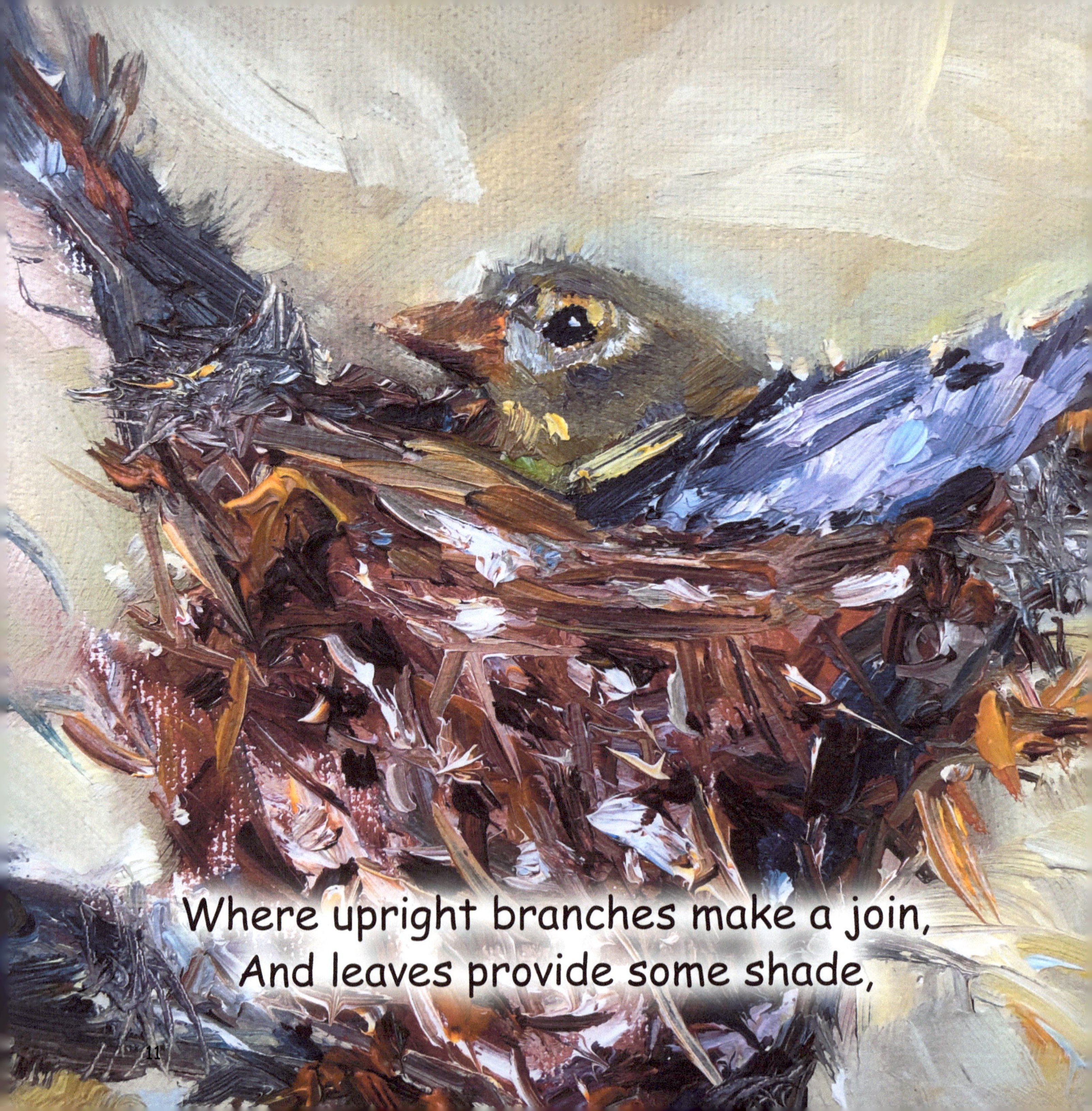

Where upright branches make a join,
And leaves provide some shade,

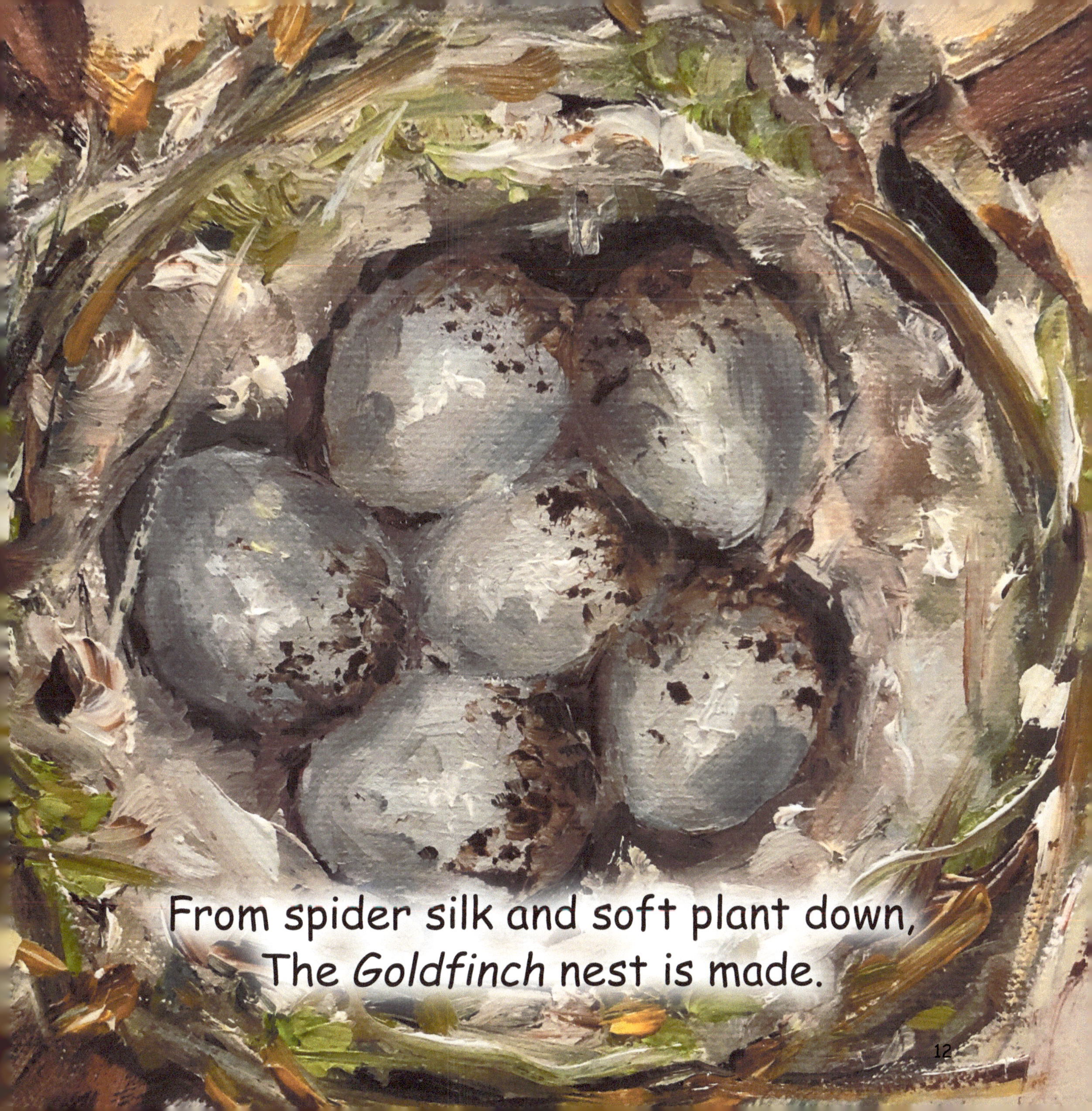

From spider silk and soft plant down,
The *Goldfinch* nest is made.

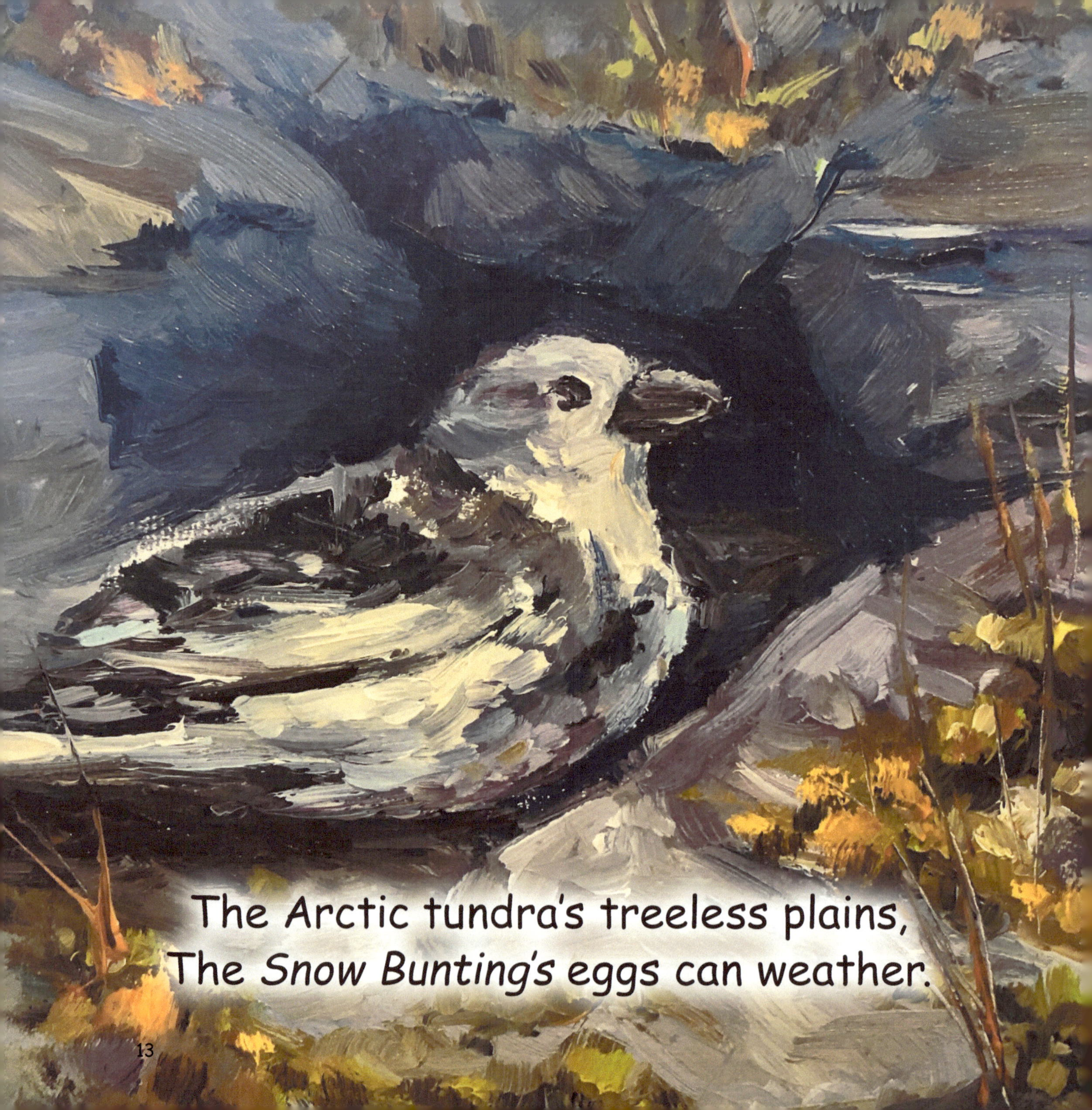

The Arctic tundra's treeless plains,
The *Snow Bunting's* eggs can weather.

13

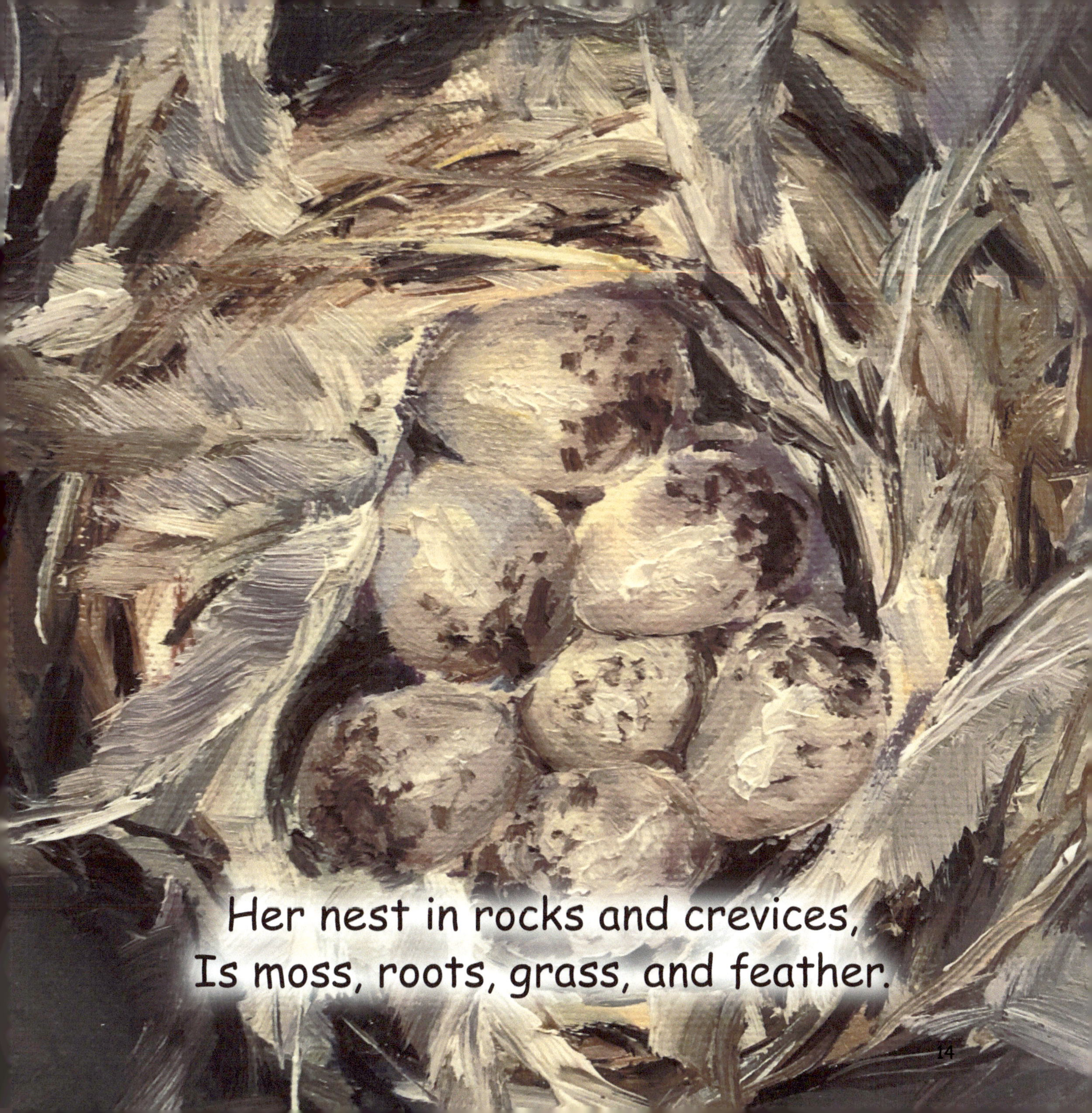
Her nest in rocks and crevices,
Is moss, roots, grass, and feather.

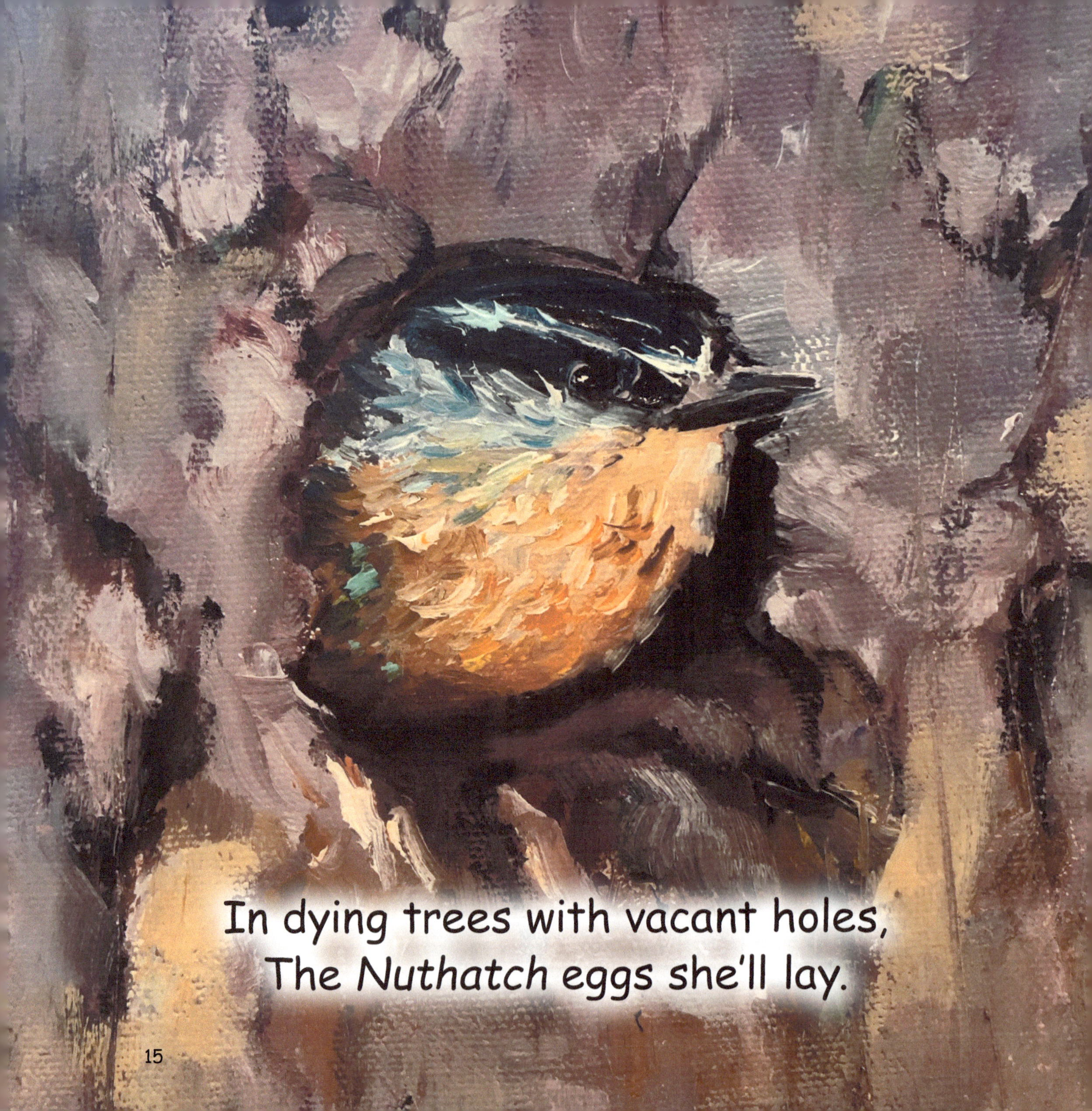
In dying trees with vacant holes,
The Nuthatch eggs she'll lay.

15

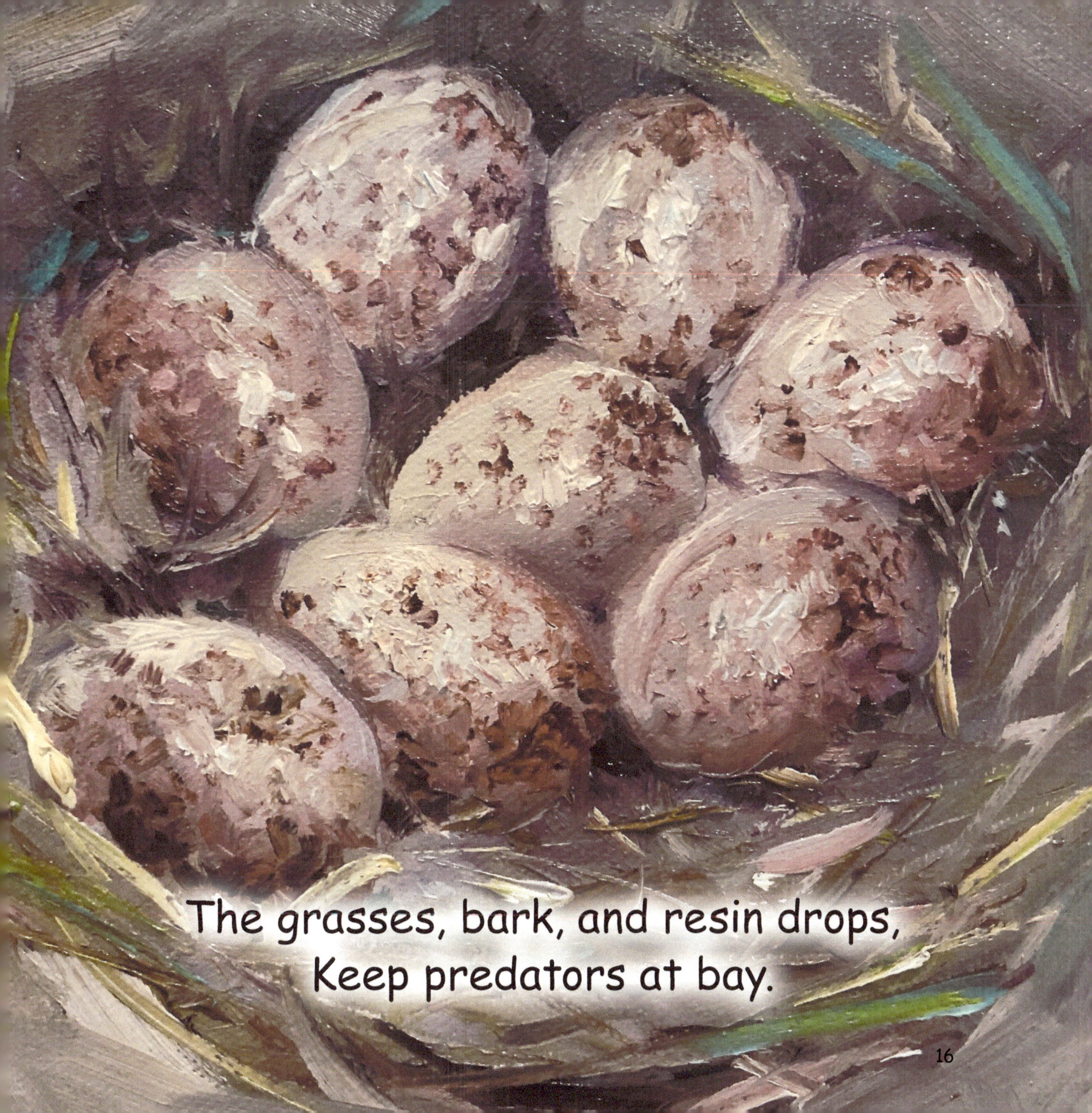

The grasses, bark, and resin drops,
Keep predators at bay.

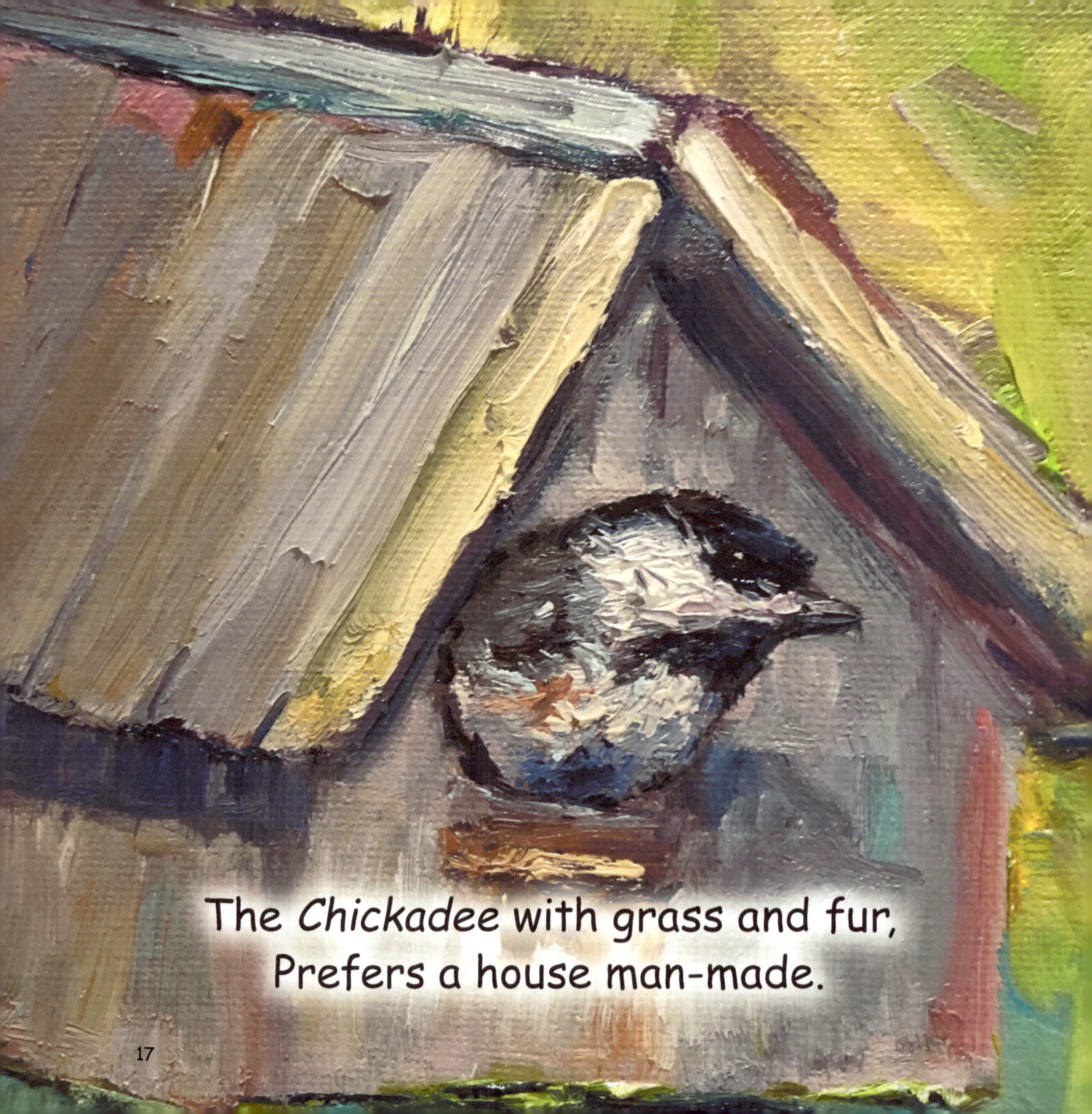

The *Chickadee* with grass and fur,
Prefers a house man-made.

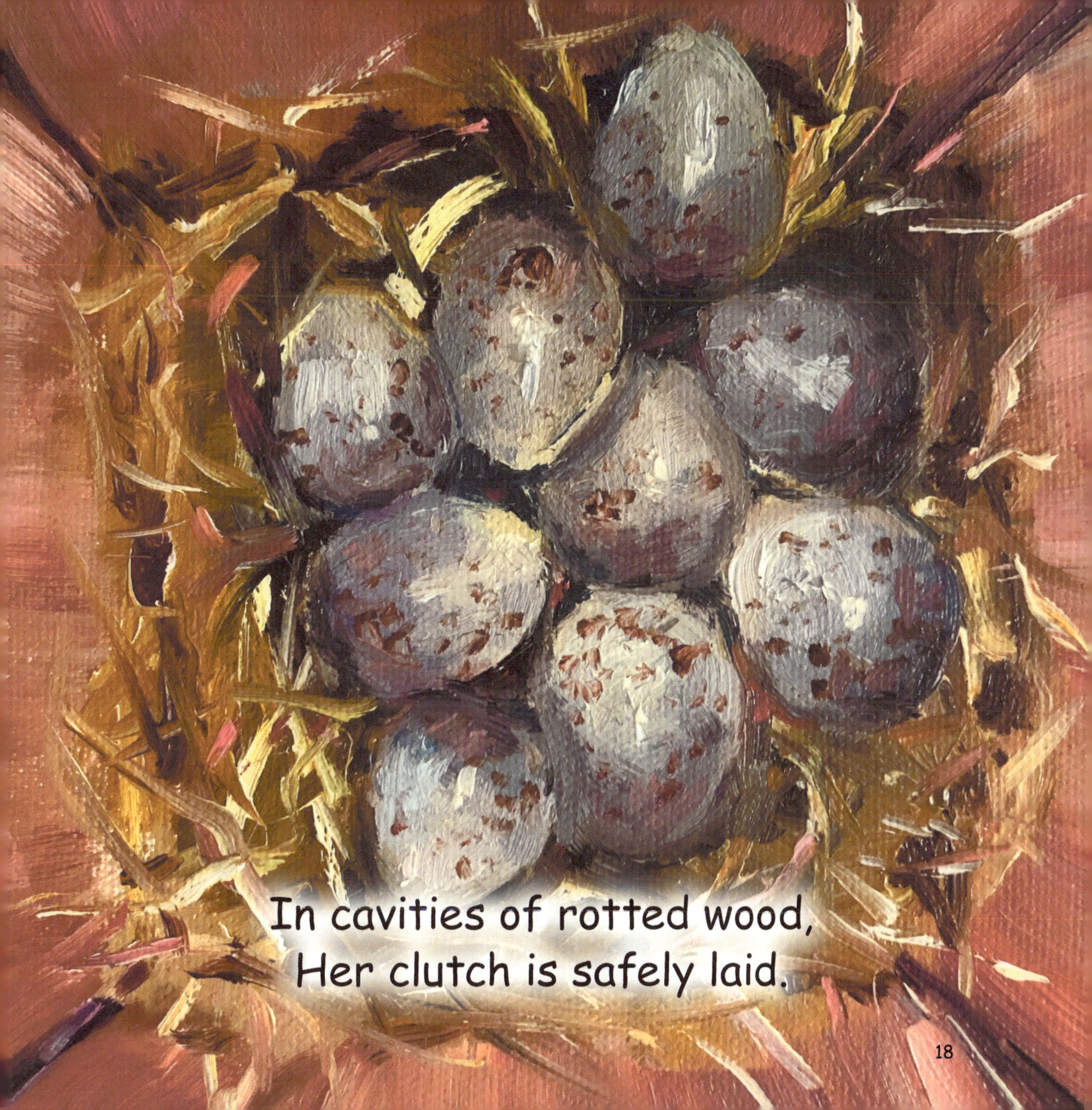

In cavities of rotted wood,
Her clutch is safely laid.

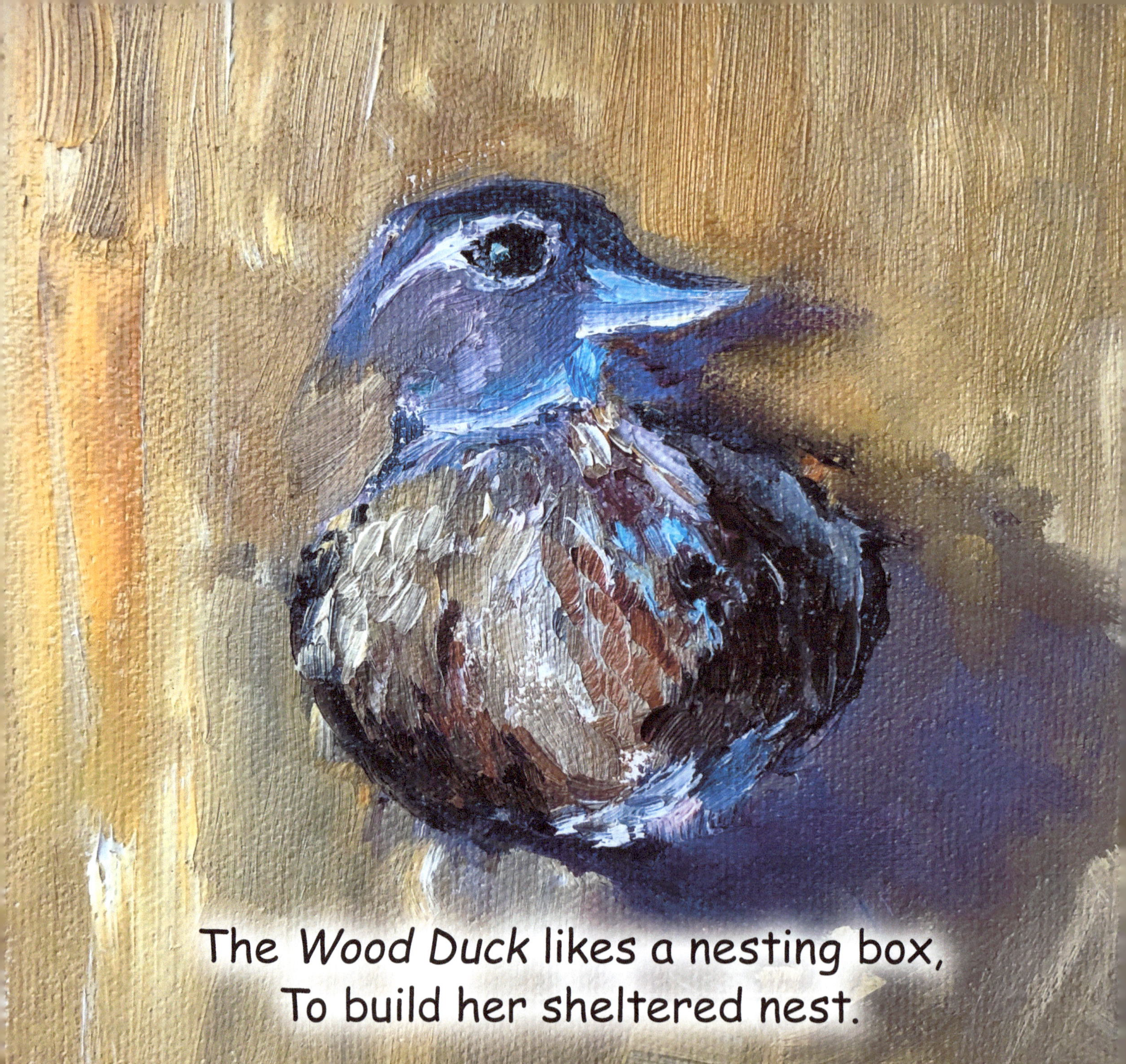

The *Wood Duck* likes a nesting box,
To build her sheltered nest.

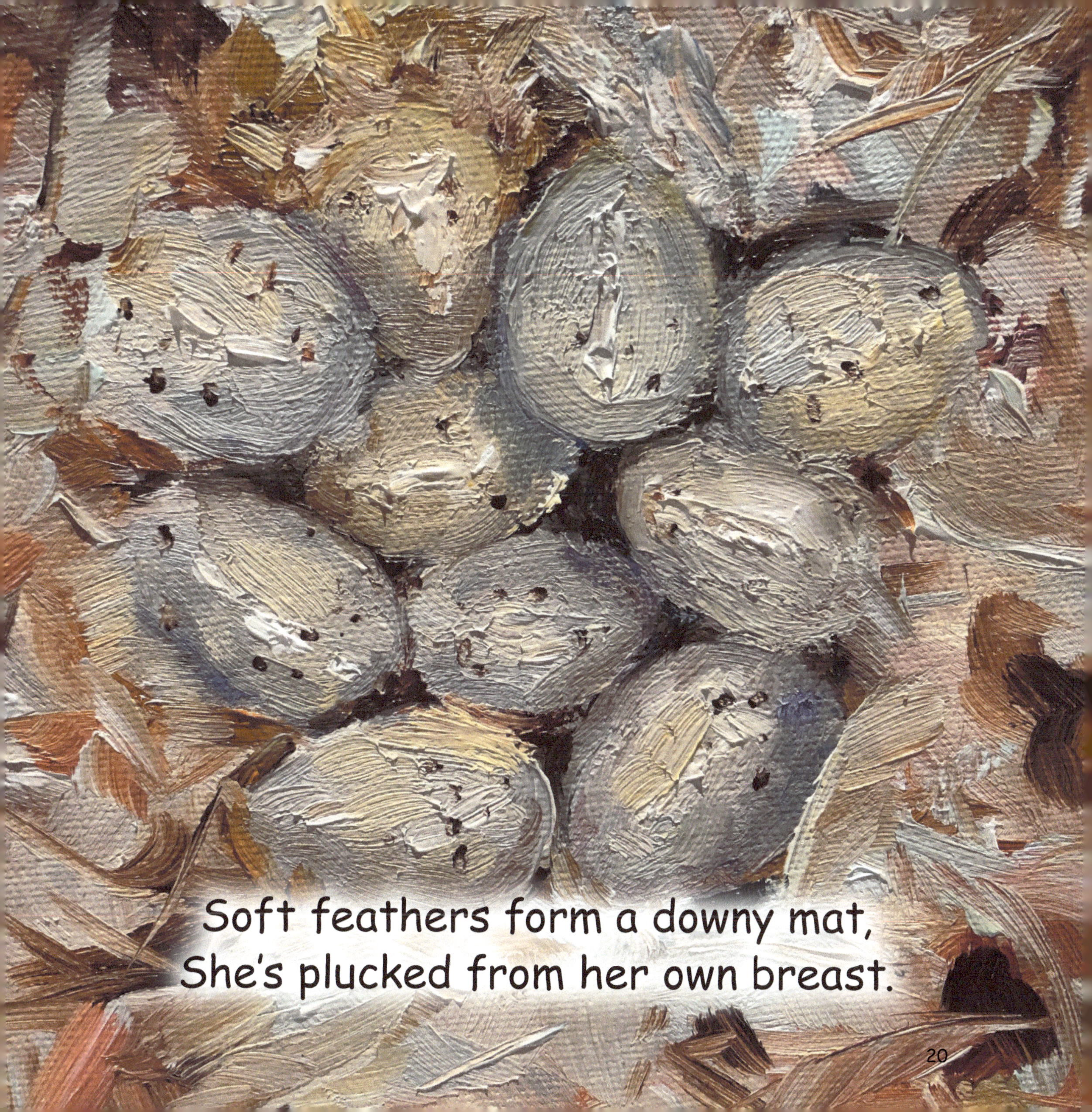

Soft feathers form a downy mat,
She's plucked from her own breast.

Paintings featured in *Nesting Grounds*:

The Tail Feathers

www.ingramcontent.com/pod-product-compliance
Lightning Source LLC
Chambersburg PA
CBHW042142030726
47599CB00002B/588